The Life and Times of

SIR WALTER RALEIGH

Mitchell Lane
PUBLISHERS

P.O. Box 196 · Hockessin, Delaware 19707

Profiles in American History

Titles in the Series

The Life and Times of

Alexander Hamilton

Benjamin Franklin

Betsy Ross

Eli Whitney

George Rogers Clark

Hernando Cortés

John Adams

John Cabot

John Hancock

John Peter Zenger

Nathan Hale

Patrick Henry

Paul Revere

Samuel Adams

Sir Walter Raleigh

Susan B. Anthony

Thomas Jefferson

William Penn

Profiles in American History

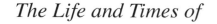

The Life and Times of

SIR WALTER RALEIGH

Earle Rice Jr.

Printing   1   2   3   4   5   6   7   8   9

Library of Congress Cataloging-in-Publication Data
Rice, Earle.
   The life and times of Sir Walter Raleigh / by Earle Rice, Jr.
      p. cm. — (Profiles in American history)
   Includes bibliographical references and index.
   ISBN 1-58415-452-7 (lib. bound : alk. paper)
   1. Raleigh, Walter, Sir, 1552?–1618—Juvenile literature. 2. Great Britain—Court and courtiers—Biography—Juvenile literature. 3. Explorers—Great Britain—Biography—Juvenile literature. I. Title. II. Series.
DA86.22.R2R36 2006
942.05'5092—dc22   2005028501

ISBN-10: 1-58415-452-7   ISBN-13: 9781584154525

ABOUT THE AUTHOR: Earle Rice Jr. is a former senior design engineer and technical writer in the aerospace industry. He has devoted full time to his writing since 1993. He has written more than fifty books for young adults. Rice is listed in *Who's Who in America* and is a member of the Society of Children's Book Writers and Illustrators, the League of World War I Aviation Historians and its UK-based sister organization, Cross & Cockade International, the United States Naval Institute, the Air Force Association, and the Disabled American Veterans. He lives in the mountains of Southern California with his wife, daughter, two granddaughters, and four cats.

PHOTO CREDITS: Cover, pp. 6, 17—National Portrait Gallery; pp. 1, 20, 28, 34, 36—Library of Congress; p. 12—National Maritime Museum; p. 25—Sharon Beck; p. 33—Johne Makin.

PUBLISHER'S NOTE: This story is based on the author's extensive research, which he believes to be accurate. Documentation of such research is contained on page 46.

   The internet sites referenced herein were active as of the publication date. Due to the fleeting nature of some web sites, we cannot guarantee they will all be active when you are reading this book.

PLB

Profiles in American History

Contents

Chapter One
    Prisoner of the King..7
    *FYInfo: The Tower of London................................. 11
Chapter Two
    Early Life and Fortune 13
    FYInfo: Good Queen Bess...................................... 19
Chapter Three
    Favorite at Court 21
    FYInfo: The Lost Colony 27
Chapter Four
    Adventurer at Large 29
    FYInfo: The Spanish Armada 35
Chapter Five
    Even Stars Must Fall..37
    FYI Info: The Plots Against the King 42
Chapter Notes 43
Chronology.. 44
Timeline in History.. 45
Further Reading 46
    For Young Adults... 46
    Works Consulted 46
    On the Internet.. 46
Glossary...47
Index 48
*For Your Information

Sir Walter Raleigh was captain of the Queen's Guard. He is wearing the "Green Greenwich" armor, typical of the armor worn by fashionable young men of his day. The armor is exhibited today in the Tower of London.

CHAPTER 1

Prisoner of the King

On November 17, 1603, Sir Walter Raleigh stood before the King's Bench at Wolvesey Castle in Winchester, England. A half-century of adventurous living had flecked his hair with gray and robbed his spirit of vitality. He stood accused of treasons against the crown, charges he vigorously denied. His trial lasted but a single day. A jury of his peers returned a verdict in fifteen minutes: GUILTY! Sir John Popham, the Lord Chief Justice, put on his black cap and read the horrid sentence:

> That you shall be led from hence to the place whence you came, there to remain until the day of execution; and from thence you shall be drawn upon a hurdle [a frame or sled] through the open streets to the place of execution, there to be hanged and cut down alive, and your body shall be opened, your heart and bowels plucked out . . . then your head to be stricken off from your body, and your body shall be divided into four quarters, to be disposed of at the King's pleasure. And God have mercy upon your soul.[1]

Raleigh showed no emotion when he learned his fate. He asked the seven government commissioners at trial to appeal to King James I for leniency on his behalf. As a former Captain of the

Queen's Guard, he had witnessed many such executions. Surely, he said, a man of his rank deserves a less grisly, more honorable kind of death. He did not plead for his life to be spared. He knew that the wages for convicted traitors was almost always death. Instead, death with honor became the theme of his remaining days.

On November 18, 1603, prosecutors tried three more principals in the alleged conspiracy against the crown—Lord Cobham (Henry Brooke), Lord Thomas Grey, and Sir Griffin Markham. A jury returned guilty verdicts for all three. The Lord Chief Justice sentenced them to be hanged, drawn, and quartered on Friday, December 10. For reasons yet unclear, Raleigh's sentence was set for the following Monday.

Cold and drizzle ushered in the wintry morning of December 10. At ten o'clock, Sir Griffin Markham was escorted to the specially erected scaffold in the courtyard of the Royal Castle of Winchester. Sir Griffin, a professional swordsman for hire, was to become the first of the three conspirators to part with his head. He bid farewell to his friends, knelt and said his prayers, then waited for the executioner's ax to drop. At that moment, Sir Benjamin Tichbourne, the sheriff, stayed the execution with a last-second reprieve from King James I.

Lord Thomas Grey, a radical Puritan (Protestant), followed Sir Griffin to the scaffold. The dapper lord looked cheerful. To officials and onlookers, he claimed only small fault in the plot against the king. He prayed for half an hour. As before, the sheriff held off the ax man at the last possible moment with another reprieve.

Lord Cobham, the chief conspirator, mounted the scaffold next. He repented his offenses against the king. Most important, he swore that all his testimony against Raleigh was true "upon hope of his soul's ressurection."[2] Again the sheriff intervened. Cobham was spared.

The king had won at a deadly game of trickery. He had signed the death warrants of the three convicted conspirators on December 8. On December 7, however, he had secretly issued reprieves for them. Only his messenger knew of their existence. The crafty monarch had hoped to draw affirmations of Raleigh's role in the plot against him. Men facing the executioner's ax, he thought, would

surely speak the truth. Once Lord Cobham spoke out against Sir Walter, the king had accomplished his deceitful aim. Immediately afterward, the sheriff brought Markham and Grey back to the scaffold. All three conspirators publicly affirmed their fair trials and treatment and deplored their crimes. The sheriff then stepped forward and declared: "See the mercy of your Prince, who of himself hath sent hither a countermand, and hath given you your lives."[3] The onlooking crowd burst into cheers that carried all the way to town.

Throughout the spectacle, Sir Walter watched the proceedings from his quarters in a castle tower overlooking the courtyard. He did not know what to make of the reprieves. Neither could he know how the "mercy" of the king would affect his own appointment with the executioner three days hence. He conducted himself accordingly: he prepared himself to die. On Sunday night—the night before his scheduled execution—he penned a final letter to his beloved wife, Elizabeth. "You shall now receive (my deare wife) my last words in these last lines," he began. "My love I send you that you may keep it when I am dead, and my councell that you may remember it when I am no more."[4]

Sir Walter went on to write many things during the eve of what he thought to be his final departure. He sent his thanks for her care and many sacrifices. She should not mourn his passing but bury her grief with him in the dust. His failure to leave her in no better estate saddened him. She should further disdain material things and not trouble herself with worldly concerns. Rather, she should place her trust in her faith, for the world's real riches lie within. Take care of their son, he implored, leaving a list of small debts owed to him.

Nearing the end of his letter, he apologized for leaving her and the boy. He despised death and leaving his loved ones, but he could not bring himself to beg for his life lest his son know him as something less than a man. He hoped for the forgiveness of his persecutors and false accusers in the afterlife. And at last he wrote his farewell. "Written with the dying hand of sometimes thy husband, but now alasse overthrowne," he concluded. "Yours that was, but now not my own. Walter Rawleigh."[5]

Raleigh's quarters in the Bloody Tower. Sir Walter was confined for thirteen years in the Tower of London, largely in the Bloody Tower. During these years, he devoted much of his time to scientific studies and experiments and to his writing.

The next morning, Sir Walter received news that King James I had stayed his execution. He was to be returned instead to his quarters in the Bloody Tower in the Tower of London. (His trial had been moved to Winchester, thirty miles to the south, because the plague was rampant in London at the time.) Sir Walter Raleigh would remain a prisoner there—"at the King's pleasure"[6]—for the next thirteen years.

The Tower of London

The Tower of London—or simply the Tower—is a royal fortress that stands on the north bank of the Thames River in London, England. William the Conqueror began erecting fortifications at the site immediately after he was crowned on Christmas 1066. He wanted to control access to the Upper Pool of London, the city's major port area at the time. In 1078, construction began on the central keep (stronghold). Built of white limestone, the keep became known as the White Tower. It provided the nucleus for a series of concentric defenses. The defense rings enclose an inner and outer ward or court.

The Wakefield and Bloody Towers

The inner ring or "curtain" surrounds the White Tower and contains thirteen additional towers. The best known of these towers are the Bloody Tower, the Beauchamp Tower, and the Wakefield Tower. Sir Walter Raleigh lived in two rooms on the second floor of the Bloody Tower for most of his thirteen-year confinement. The outer curtain is surrounded by a moat (now drained). A protective wall beyond the moat contains multiple embrasures for cannon. The sprawling complex occupies eighteen acres. Historically, the Tower has been used as a royal palace, a prison and execution place, an arsenal, a royal mint, a menagerie, and a public records office.

Today, only a single land gate at the Tower's southwest corner provides access to the complex. The thirteenth-century water gate on the Thames once received heavy use when the river served as a major highway. Called the Traitors' Gate, it took its nickname from the prisoners brought through it when the Tower was used as a prison.

Some of the famous persons executed at the Tower include statesman Edmund Dudley (1510); humanist Sir Thomas More (1535); and Anne Boleyn, the second wife of Henry VIII (1536). Executions generally took place on Tower Green or Tower Hill.

For Your Information

Philip II and Mary I. Mary was the daughter of Henry VIII and Catherine of Aragon. When Mary I ("Bloody Mary") succeeded her brother Edward VI to the throne in 1553, she married Philip II of Spain and restored Catholicism as England's state religion.

CHAPTER 2

Early Life and Fortune

Walter Raleigh was born at Hayes Barton, a family home in Devon, England. The year of his birth was probably 1554, but possibly 1552. Local birth records were not kept until April 1555. Accordingly, his exact birth date remains uncertain. His father, also named Walter, was a merchant and gentleman farmer. The old and respected Raleigh family had lived in England's West Country for two centuries. Although the family name and fortune had declined a little over the years, Walter senior still managed to support his family comfortably.

The elder Walter Raleigh married three times. His first wife, Joan Drake, was cousin to Francis Drake, the famous sailor. Her marriage to Raleigh yielded two sons, John and George. Joan died in the late 1530s. Raleigh next married the daughter of a merchant from either Genoa or London. She died giving birth to a daughter named Mary in the 1540s.

About 1549, Raleigh married his third wife, Katherine Champernowne Gilbert. Katherine was the daughter of Devon nobility and the widow of Otho Gilbert, who had owned Compton and Greenway Castles. Their union produced three sons, John, Humphrey, and Adrian Gilbert. In her marriage to Raleigh, Katherine bore her spouse a daughter, Margaret—or Margery—and two more sons, Carew and young Walter Raleigh.

Young Walter entered the world at a time of religious unrest in England. About twenty years before he was born, Rome had refused to annul Henry VIII's marriage to Catherine of Aragon. The angry king responded by breaking with the Roman Catholic Church. In its place, he established the Protestant Church of England. Henry installed himself at its head. His son and successor, Edward VI, carried on Henry's Protestant legacy during his reign (1547–1553). Both Walter senior and Katherine became strong Protestant believers. Many people in the region chose to remain Catholic. Religious tensions began to build among neighbors.

When Henry's first daughter (by Catherine) succeeded Edward to the throne as Mary I ("Bloody Mary") in 1553, she married Philip II of Spain. Mary immediately restored the Catholic faith as the state religion in England. As a result, many Protestants suffered abuse and violence at the hands of Catholics. The Raleighs proved no exception.

Young Walter's family endured many injustices in the name of religion. They witnessed the hanging of the Vicar of St. Thomas from his church tower in Exeter. And Katherine put her own life at risk to console Agnes Prest in prison. Devon authorities had arrested Agnes, a simple Protestant gentlewoman, for heresy. Catholic villagers burned Agnes at the stake the next day. Walter, who would gain future fame as a soldier, navigator, explorer, poet, scholar, and courtier, learned early in life to hate Catholics.

History has revealed little of Walter's youth. Accounts of his life usually skim over his boyhood years. Details of his early life begin in 1569, when he was about fifteen. That year, he joined his relative, Henry Champernowne, and a group of volunteers, to fight with the Huguenots (French Protestants) in France's Third War of Religion (1568–1570). Based on his later reference to the March 1569 battle of Jarnac (in his *History of the World*) he did not distinguish himself in the fighting. The Catholics defeated the ill-prepared Huguenot army and forced its retreat. During the fray, they also captured and shot one of the chief Protestant commanders, Louis de Bourbon, the famed Prince of Condé. Walter later credited the reckless prince's end to his "being over-confident in his own courage."[1] During several years in France, Walter took part in numerous battles against

the French Catholics, including the battles of Moncontour and Languedoc. And he narrowly missed the St. Bartholomew's Day Massacre (August 24–25, 1572), which eventually took the lives of some three thousand Huguenots in Paris. Tens of thousands more were killed in the provinces.

Upon his return from France, Walter gained admittance to Oriel College, Oxford, probably in 1572. He left Oriel without a degree after three years. He then studied law and debated current affairs at the Middle Temple in London in 1575. During these years, Walter was learning the ways of both a soldier and a scholar. He was bright, brave, ambitious, and endowed with a sense of destiny. His ample charm attracted friends easily. His often haughty manner created enemies with equal ease. A youthful zest for life and a

Oriel College, Oxford. Raleigh enrolled at Oriel, probably in 1572, but left without a degree after three years. He went on to study law and debate current affairs at the Middle Temple in London in 1575.

bit of the imp in him often landed him in trouble for brawling and playing practical jokes.

Physically, Walter cut a dashing figure. At age twenty-one, he stood about six feet tall in days when few men did. Dark brown hair crowned his high forehead and ovular face; while a lighter-hued mustache and beard and light brown eyes deemphasized his long, slender nose. His appearance prompted English folklorist John Aubrey to describe him as "tall, handsome and bold, with a graceful presence."[2] Aubrey added that Walter spoke in a small voice with a Devonshire accent. Some scholars look upon his accent as a hindrance to his career aspirations, but Walter's soldierly bearing and ease of movement suited well the courtier he was soon to become.

At Oriel and Middle Temple, Walter excelled in philosophy and public speaking. In addition to school, he spent endless hours in the study of his half brother Sir Humphrey Gilbert at Limehouse. He pored over the works of Aristotle and acquainted himself with his brother's writings. Walter took particular interest in Sir Humphrey's "Discourse to prove a Passage by the North-West to Cathaia [Cathay, or China] and the East Indies."

At Limehouse, Walter also met Welsh mathematician John Dee. He learned for the first time about Dee's vision for establishing a Tudor Empire in North America. (The Tudor line of English royalty began with Henry VII, father of Henry VIII.) Walter also published his first literary work in 1576—a short poem poking fun at fashionable society. The verse was credited to "Walter Rawely of the Middle Temple." (Rawely was one of more than forty variant spellings for *Raleigh*, today's preferred spelling.)

With his cousins and fellow students Charles Champernowne and George Carew, Walter met many influential people. He also made his first attempts to catch the eye of Elizabeth I. "Good Queen Bess" or the "Virgin Queen," as she was known, was the daughter of Henry VIII and his second wife, Anne Boleyn. By order of Elizabeth, who succeeded Mary I when she died in 1558, the state religion reverted to her late father's Protestant Church of England. As a seasoned soldier with a flair for poetics, Walter soon saw a future for himself at court. To gain access to the queen, he became friends with Robert Dudley, the Earl of Leicester (pronounced LEH-ster), and his nephew, Sir Philip Sydney. Both men ranked high in Elizabeth's esteem. Even so, it was Walter's brother and mentor, Sir Humphrey, who most influenced his early life.

In 1578, relations between England and Spain had reached a new low. A near crisis arose from privateering raids on Spanish shipping and ports in the New World by Sir Francis Drake and other English "Sea Rovers." (Privateers like Drake were basically state-sanctioned pirates.) Philip II of Spain (husband of the late Mary I) called on Elizabeth I to stop the looting of Spanish ships and ports, but the queen's depleted treasury needed the infusion of Philip's gold. When Elizabeth failed to act, Philip became increasingly more frustrated. War seemed imminent.

Sir Humphrey Gilbert saw the chance to use the deepening crisis to his advantage. He planned a voyage of discovery to the New World. Walter's visionary brother imagined how English colonies in the Americas would rival those of Spain. For this purpose, he obtained a letter patent from the queen. (A letter patent is an offi-

Robert Dudley, Earl of Leicester, was a favorite of Elizabeth I and one of her numerous suitors. He failed to win her hand in marriage but remained a loyal friend to the queen throughout his life.

cial document conferring a right or privilege.) The letter authorized Sir Humphrey to "discover and take possession of any remote, barbarous and heathen lands not possessed by any Christian prince or people."[3]

Sir Humphrey assembled a small fleet of seven vessels and 409 men, with himself as admiral aboard the flagship *Anne Aucher*. He invited Walter to join the expedition as captain of the 100-ton *Falcon*. As preparations for the voyage moved forward, three vessels left the fleet over quarrels between Sir Humphrey and another ship's captain. Several storms then delayed the departure of the remaining ships. Sir Humphrey finally set sail with four ships in November 1578.

The reduced fleet headed first for Ireland, but another powerful gale forced three of the four ships to turn back to England. Walter sailed on in the *Falcon* and disappeared. Supposedly, he ended up in the Azores, off Portugal. In the islands, so say some reports, Walter and his men engaged in a dangerous sea battle. According to John Hooker, a friend of Walter senior, "many of [young Walter's] company were slain"[4] in a clash with Spanish warships. (The incident likely arose over an act of English piracy.)

The *Falcon* returned to Dartmouth about six months later. After the Privy Council (official advisers to the crown) reviewed Sir Humphrey's aborted voyage of discovery, it ordered both Sir Humphrey and Walter not to sail again. The queen clearly disapproved of Gilbert's bungled expedition. She thought something less of Walter's tiff with the Spaniards. At age twenty-four, young Walter's courtly aspirations had suffered a temporary setback—but fortune favors the bold of heart and deed, and Walter's fortune was soon to rise.

Good Queen Bess

Elizabeth I assumed the throne of England upon the death of her half sister, Mary I, in 1558. Born near London on September 7, 1533, Elizabeth was the daughter of Henry VIII and his second wife, Anne Boleyn. Unlike Mary, Elizabeth was raised as a Protestant. A solid classical education prepared her well for the burdens of leadership she would face. She began her reign at a time when England was weakened by war abroad and torn by religious strife at home. The treasury was empty, and France and Spain posed a continuing threat to her island nation. Ruling England in the second half of the sixteenth century was not a job for the faint of heart. Elizabeth proved she was up to the task.

While overcoming numerous attempts to unseat her from the throne—one of which resulted in the beheading of her cousin Mary, Queen of Scots—Elizabeth's accomplishments were legion: With the help of her secretary of state Sir William Cecil (later Lord Burghley), she ended the war with France; she reinstated the Protestant Church of England as the state church without provoking a religious rebellion; she supported the Protestant Dutch in their fight against the Catholic Spaniards; she stood against Philip II of Spain and sent her fleet to destroy his Grand Armada; and she powered England into a major European force in politics, commerce, and the arts.

Elizabeth entertained many suitors, including Sir Walter Raleigh and Essex, but she never married. Her choice to remain single earned her the byname of the Virgin Queen. Her loving and devoted subjects knew her best as Good Queen Bess. The years of her reign (1558–1603) became known as the Golden Age or the Elizabethan Age.

For Your Information

Mary, Queen of Scots. Originally named Mary Stuart (or Stewart), she was the daughter of James V of Scotland and his French wife Mary of Guise. As the grand-niece of Henry VIII, she posed a threat to the English throne, so Mary I ("Bloody Mary") ordered her beheading.

CHAPTER
3

Favorite at Court

Raleigh returned to England from the Azores in 1579. He needed some way of showing the queen his still untapped abilities. The Irish rebellion against English rule in 1580 offered him a chance to prove himself. At age twenty-six, he took a commission as a captain in the British Army and went off to Ireland with a hundred foot soldiers.

It was a barbaric time in Anglo-Irish relations. The queen named Lord Thomas Grey of Wilton as lord deputy of Ireland. She asked him to put down the revolt. Sir Humphrey Gilbert took an active role in the cruel suppression. He burned villages and massacred many soldiers and civilians.

His brother Walter Raleigh was with him. In what would be called the Smerwick Massacre, Raleigh coldly slaughtered 300 Italian and Spanish mercenaries (soldiers for hire) who had already surrendered to Lord Grey. He also fought off a large force with his pistol to save a fallen friend. Time and again, he conducted himself bravely in the eyes of his men, winning their respect.

Raleigh hated serving under Lord Grey. He thought the lord's policies worked against English interests. Lord Grey did not like Raleigh, either. Inevitably, their personalities clashed. Raleigh wanted to return to court in England. He wrote to the Earl of Leicester for his assistance: "I have spent some time here under the Deputy

[Grey], in such poor place and charge as, were it not that I knew him to be one of yours, I would disdain it as much as to keep sheep."[1]

At about the same time, Lord Grey wrote to England's secretary of state, Sir Francis Walsingham, about Captain Raleigh: "For my own part, I must be plain: I neither like his carriage nor his company."[2] A short while later, Walsingham sent a letter recalling Raleigh to England. Captain Raleigh returned home in late 1581.

Back in England, Raleigh continued to criticize Lord Grey's policies. Folklorist John Aubrey, reporting on courtly gossip, wrote that Raleigh "told his tale so well, and with so good a grace and presence, that the Queen took especial notice of him and presently preferred him."[3] Raleigh had caught Elizabeth's ear—and her eye.

One popular tale about Raleigh's "grace and presence" continues to endure. He is said to have gallantly swept off his cloak and spread it over a mud puddle so that the queen could walk across it without soiling her shoes. The incident probably never happened, but it accurately depicts the image he projected. In any case, his sharp wit and handsome figure captured Elizabeth's fancy. Early in their relationship, Raleigh recognized how shaky his standing was at court. Any misstep could cause his fall from grace. Aware of this, he fingered a poem on a windowpane at the queen's Greenwich Palace. "Fain [willingly] would I climb, yet I fear to fall," he began. Elizabeth completed the couplet: "If thy heart fail thee, climb not at all."[4] Walter climbed. He would remain at court for the next ten years as one of the queen's favorites.

Elizabeth showered Walter with favors and lavish gifts, including a lease to Durham House, one of London's fanciest homes. Later, she gave him two impressive estates she had received as gifts from All Souls College, Oxford. For services rendered, she awarded him 42,000 acres of land in Ireland. The land included beautiful castles at Lismore (near Cork) and Waterford. He would eventually introduce the potato to Ireland and attempt to farm tobacco there.

Of even greater importance, the queen conferred upon Raleigh numerous trade licenses and monopolies—wine, textiles, and more. He also benefited from privateering investments. Once, in explaining the difference between privateers and pirates, Raleigh commented, "Did you ever know of any that were pirates for mil-

lions? They only that work for small things are pirates."[5] His commercial interests alone soon yielded an equivalent of close to a million dollars a year. Enormously wealthy, he served his guests on silver-plated dinnerware engraved with his coat of arms.

On June 11, 1583, Sir Humphrey Gilbert, with Elizabeth's renewed permission, sailed west again with a small fleet of five ships. Raleigh did not sail with him this time. Gilbert wanted to fulfill his dream of founding English colonies in the New World before his letter patent from the queen ran out the next year.

This voyage was again plagued from the start and ended in tragedy. Sir Humphrey reached Newfoundland in August and claimed the land for Queen Elizabeth (even though John Cabot had already claimed it for England in 1497). But on his return voyage, he perished in monstrous seas near the Azores. One of his captains heard him shout these now-famous words: "We are as near to heaven by sea as by land." Soon afterward, the captain reported, Sir Humphrey's ship "was devoured and swallowed up of the sea."[6]

Raleigh took over his brother's passion to establish English colonies in the new land. Elizabeth granted him a letter patent for that purpose. To her delight, he named the land Virginia (for her nickname, the Virgin Queen). Although he would never set foot in Virginia, he financed a series of expeditions to the new land. Supposedly, the several voyages were to settle colonists. Actually, they were to look for gold and silver mines in the Americas.

Raleigh's attempts to colonize Virginia ended unsuccessfully with the mysterious disappearance of 117 settlers on Roanoke Island. The vanished settlement gained renown as the "Lost Colony." Walter's "colonizing" investments netted him losses of about 40,000 pounds, a sizable sum at the time. His riches otherwise continued to mount, however, as did his standing at court.

In 1585, Elizabeth knighted him for his colonizing efforts. As Sir Walter Raleigh, he continued to receive prestigious rankings from his admiring monarch. She appointed him warden of the stannaries (tin mines), lieutenant of Cornwall, and vice admiral of Devon and Cornwall. Sir Walter served his queen well. Along with Sir Francis Walsingham, he became a spymaster of sorts. Together, the two knights helped uncover the Babington Plot in 1586. The plot was a Catholic scheme to assassinate Elizabeth and replace her with Mary, Queen of Scots. Elizabeth ordered Mary's beheading for her part in the plot. Other conspirators met similar ends. Raleigh's role in exposing the plot endeared him even more to the queen.

In 1587, Elizabeth appointed Raleigh as the new captain of the Queen's Guard. This position was significant because it required his constant attendance on the queen. Raleigh's star had reached its zenith. He would remain the queen's favorite for another two years. But with the appearance at court of Robert Devereux, 2nd Earl of Essex, Raleigh's star grew dimmer and started to decline. When he secretly married Elizabeth ("Bess") Throckmorton on November 19, 1591 (sources vary regarding the date), he put his favor in jeopardy.

Bess was the daughter of Sir Nicholas Throckmorton, Elizabeth's first ambassador to Paris. In 1584, at the age of nineteen, she appeared as a maid of honor at Elizabeth's court. Raleigh was attracted to her at once, and the two fell madly in love. In the summer of 1591, Bess became pregnant, and her marriage to Walter became a necessity. On March 29, 1592, she presented Walter with a son, Damerei, who died soon afterward. The scandalous romance of the devoted pair would soon cost them both dearly.

At age fifty-four, Elizabeth found herself irresistibly drawn to the stormy, dark-haired, dark-eyed Essex, a youth some thirty-four years her junior. Essex first drew attention fighting courageously against the Spanish in the Netherlands in 1584. Elizabeth made him master of the horse the next year. The ambitious young nobleman set out at once to replace Raleigh in the aging queen's affections.

In 1588, however, court rivalries gave way to Spain's long-threatened assault on England. On May 20, Philip II of Spain launched his Grand Armada—130 ships, 8,000 seamen, and 19,000 soldiers—in an effort to invade the island nation.

The Armada appeared off England's Lizard Point on July 29. A mixed squadron of ninety-four English ships, led by Lord Howard of Effingham, Sir Francis Drake, and others, met and defeated the Armada in a monthlong running sea battle. As vice admiral of Devon and Cornwall, Raleigh played only a minor role in preparing the island's land defenses. He felt convinced, as he later wrote, that the English were "of no such force as to encounter an Armie like unto

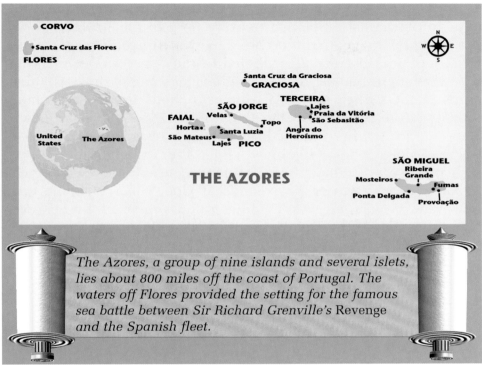

The Azores, a group of nine islands and several islets, lies about 800 miles off the coast of Portugal. The waters off Flores provided the setting for the famous sea battle between Sir Richard Grenville's Revenge and the Spanish fleet.

that [Spanish forces]."[7] Rather than engaging the Spanish on land, the English prevailed at sea.

After the defeat of the Armada, Essex resumed his efforts to replace Walter as the queen's favorite. He even challenged Raleigh to a duel for reasons unknown in December 1588, but other parties intervened. The rivalry continued. Raleigh, hoping to regain some of his lost favor, joined in a privateering expedition to the coast of Portugal in 1589. He, Drake, Essex, and others planned to provoke a Portuguese rebellion against Philip II. (Spain had annexed the neighboring nation in 1580.) The expedition failed miserably. Elizabeth spurned both Essex and Raleigh for a time.

In the autumn of 1589, Raleigh escaped the queen's ire for a few weeks with a visit to his lands in Ireland. There, he found some peace of mind renovating his castle at Lismore. During this sojourn, he developed a close friendship with English poet Edmund Spenser, who was writing The Faerie Queen at the time. Later, back in England, Raleigh helped the poet publish his masterwork.

In January 1591, Raleigh laid plans for another privateering expedition against a Spanish treasure *flota* in the Azores. (A *flota* is a fleet of merchant ships escorted by warships.) Elizabeth refused to let him go. His cousin, Sir Richard Grenville, took his place and died bravely in the last fight of the *Revenge*, one of the best known ships in the British Navy. In tribute to Grenville, Raleigh anonymously wrote *A Report of the Truth of the Fight about the Isles of Azores*. Meanwhile, Elizabeth elevated Essex to the Order of the Garter. Raleigh's fierce rival now joined him in knighthood.

Later in 1591, Raleigh was publicly accused of being an atheist, or someone who denies the existence of God. The accusations arose out of his association with a poetic group known as the School of Night. Because of the group's skeptical attitude and critical view of the Scriptures, it gained a reputation for atheism. Although Raleigh was not an atheist, the charges plagued him for many years. They also earned him further disfavor with the queen.

In 1592, Raleigh regained some favor at court. Essex had married Frances, the daughter of Walsingham and widow of poet Sir Philip Sidney, in 1590. The jealous queen rebuked him for marrying beneath himself. Elizabeth, partially out of spite for Essex, granted Raleigh a ninety-nine-year lease on Sherborne Castle in Dorset. Raleigh then left on another privateering expedition. His renewed favor at court ended abruptly, however, when Elizabeth learned of his secret marriage to Bess. She recalled Raleigh and imprisoned him and his wife in the Tower of London. Elizabeth soon relented and set them free, but she banished them both from her court.

Raleigh was bitter at first. Later, however, Elizabeth profited greatly from one of Sir Walter's privateering ventures. She grudgingly allowed him and Bess to start life anew at Sherborne Castle. Walter and Bess retired to the Sherborne estate in Dorset. In October 1593, Bess bore him a son, christened Walter but known as Wat. Sir Walter settled into the tranquil life of a country gentleman. With time on his hands, he served in Parliament, where he often spoke on religious matters and the need for a powerful navy.

It didn't take Raleigh long to tire of the pastoral life. Almost inevitably, his thoughts returned to the vast new lands that lay far beyond the western horizon. His days as favorite at Elizabeth's court were over. His days as adventurer-at-large were about to begin.

The Lost Colony

In April 1584, Sir Walter Raleigh sent Captains Philip Amadas and Arthur Barlowe on an exploratory voyage to North America. The captains landed in present-day North Carolina in July and returned to England in September. They reported finding an abundance of fertile land, fish, game, and friendly native peoples on Roanoke Island. Raleigh spent the winter organizing and financing a colonizing expedition for the spring.

In April 1585, Raleigh sent a colony of 108 persons to the island that Amadas and Barlowe had seen only in midsummer. He appointed Sir Richard Grenville as commander of the expedition and Ralph Lane to govern the new colony. A severe winter and increasing threats of Native American attacks took their toll on the colonists. When privateer Sir Francis Drake paid a call to the island in June 1586, the 103 surviving settlers hastily decided to return to England with him. Raleigh tried again the following spring.

This time, Raleigh sent 117 colonists to Roanoke Island under the leadership of John White, a member of the first expedition. They established a second colony on the island, with White as governor. On August 18, 1587, his daughter gave birth to Virginia Dare, the first English child born in North America. Later that month, White returned to England to implore Raleigh to send more colonists and supplies to the island. Before he could return to Roanoke, Spain's Grand (or Great) Armada attacked England.

When White finally made it back to the island, he found no trace of the colony. Everyone had disappeared. The disappearance of the settlers gave rise to the longstanding and haunting American mystery known as the Lost Colony of Roanoke. Today, scholars generally believe the lost colonists intermingled with and perhaps married some Native Americans. In any event, they were never seen again.

In 1792, to honor Sir Walter Raleigh's attempt to settle the area, the city of Raleigh was chartered to serve as the capital of North Carolina.

Old Fort Raleigh on Roanoke Island, North Carolina

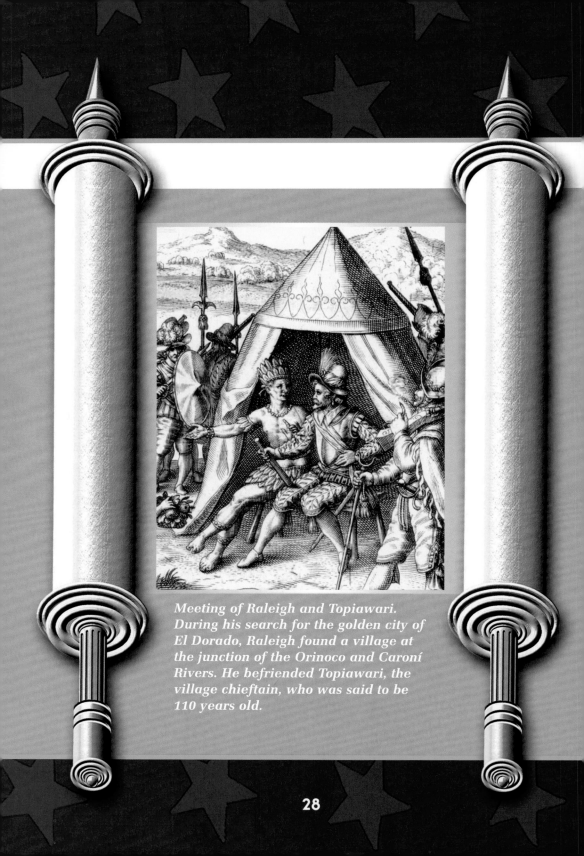

Meeting of Raleigh and Topiawari. During his search for the golden city of El Dorado, Raleigh found a village at the junction of the Orinoco and Caroní Rivers. He befriended Topiawari, the village chieftain, who was said to be 110 years old.

CHAPTER
4

Adventurer at Large

Walter Raleigh was born to adventure. He also possessed a sharp mind and a yen for prestige and power. At the time of his expulsion from court, rumors abounded in the kingdom about a legendary city of gold in South America. As the story went, the city was ruled by a rich king who had been covered with gold dust so many times he had become permanently gilded. The fabled city was called El Dorado, which means "The Golden" in Spanish. Raleigh's nimble mind formed a plan to find El Dorado and claim it for the queen. He expected thereby to regain his place at court. He began preparing for the voyage in 1594.

On February 6, 1595, he set sail for South America with a tiny fleet of four ships and a group of 300 sailors and gentlemen of adventure. Notable among the adventurers was Lawrence Keymis, an Oxford mathematician. The fleet arrived in Trinidad (off the coast of present-day Venezuela) in March. During a monthlong stay to load fresh supplies, Raleigh repaid past Spanish injustices to English seafarers: He and his men wiped out the harbor guard at Port of Spain and burned the inland town of St. Joseph. Raleigh did not want to leave any enemies at his back.

Raleigh left Trinidad with several additional vessels in his fleet and headed for the Orinoco River. He also brought along Don Antonio de Berrio, the seventy-four-year-old Spanish governor of

the island. Berrio, a veteran soldier, had led several expeditions up the Orinoco. Raleigh hoped he would lead them to El Dorado. Several local guides soon proved of little use, but the party struggled on upstream against the current.

One day, during a meal stop on the riverbank, Raleigh found an Indian basket in the bushes. It contained a refiner's materials for testing metals "and also the dust of such [gold] ore as he had refined."[1] The discovery lifted the spirits of Raleigh and his rapidly tiring men, and they labored on. In another three weeks, they reached the junction of the Orinoco and Caroní Rivers. There, they found a village ruled by an old chief named Topiawari (toh-pee-ah-WAHR-ee). He was said to be 110 years old. While making friends with Topiawari, Walter sent out scouting parties. They returned with stories of treasures untold. "Every stone that we stooped to take up," they said, "promised either gold or silver."[2] But their tales were exaggerated, and the stones proved worthless.

Shortly thereafter, torrential rainstorms set in. The downpours forced Raleigh to call off the expedition and return to England. He brought Topiawari's son with him. He also left two of his men behind in Guiana, in South America. He wanted them to learn the language and more about the area. The adventurous knight was already thinking about a return trip.

Raleigh decided to cap off his voyage to Guiana with a raid on the Spanish port at Cumaná on the Venezuelan coast. With loot from Cumaná, he might avoid returning home empty-handed. During his attack on the port, he lost four men. Twenty-seven more party members died of disease aboard ship. After the fighting, Raleigh exchanged former governor Berrio for a wounded Englishman—but he came away with no plunder. Disillusioned, he turned homeward. His vision of English colonies in the New World to surpass those of Spain would again have to wait.

Back in England, Raleigh reported on his expedition in a lengthy work entitled *The Discoverie of the Large, Rich, and Bewtiful Empyre of Guiana, with Relation of the Great and Golden Citie of Manoa* (the Indian name for El Dorado). Near the end of his report, he appealed to the queen to send a small army to claim Manoa. The golden city, he wrote, "would yield to Her Majesty . . . so many

hundred thousand pounds yearly, as should both defend [against] all enemies abroad, and defray all expenses at home."[3] Raleigh left little doubt as to his availability to lead a second expedition to Guiana. For the immediate future, however, more pressing circumstances would demand his services elsewhere.

Despite the devastating English defeat of Philip's Grand Armada in 1588, England still felt threatened by Spain. In November 1595, three months after Raleigh's return from Guiana, news reached England of another huge Spanish fleet gathering in Cadíz. Rumors ran rampant about Philip's intended invasion of Ireland. Recent burnings of Mousehole and Penzance in Cornwall by Spanish sea raiders alarmed Raleigh. Devon and Cornwall were still his responsibility. He wrote warning letters to his friend Robert Cecil, the queen's principal secretary, and to the Privy Council. After a number of lengthy delays, the queen finally decided to send a naval squadron to Spain. As Raleigh so concisely put it, "Expedition in a little is better than much too late."[4] Better to act too soon than too late, he reasoned.

A formidable English fleet began assembling. Elizabeth fitted out 96 armed ships and her Dutch allies added 24 more. Roughly 1,500 sailors manned the ships and up to 8,000 soldiers formed the landing parties. The queen appointed Lord Admiral Howard and the fiery Essex as joint generals of the enterprise. Howard had led the English triumph over Spain's Grand Armada. Essex had battled the Spaniards in the Netherlands in 1593. The two joint commanders divided the fleet into four squadrons and named Sir Francis Vere marshal of the army. Raleigh took command of a squadron of 22 ships. The fleet put to sea from Plymouth on June 1, 1596, and anchored off Cadíz 20 days later.

Despite long weeks of planning, the fleet was badly organized, and the command structure invited chaos. And chaos is precisely what it spawned.

Instead of attacking the harbor, the aging and overly cautious Howard offloaded his troops too soon. Most of the heavily armed and equipped soldiers perished when the little landing boats capsized under their weight. Meanwhile, the wildly impulsive Essex attempted to land his troops on the wrong side of Cadíz. Only Raleigh's intervention saved them from extinction. As the battle

The Spanish Grand Armada of 130 warships sailed into the English Channel on July 29, 1588. Its mission was to land an invasion force in England sent by Philip II of Spain. A smaller English fleet chased Philip's Armada into Calais harbor and attacked the Spaniards with fire ships.

went on, it was he who revised their battle plan and saved the day for the English. Raleigh, aboard his warship *Warspite*, led the last assault on the Spanish warships that had destroyed his cousin Grenville's *Revenge*. Rushing to the attack, Raleigh grimly declared his resolve "to be revenged for the *Revenge*, or to second her with mine own life."[5]

At the height of battle, he fell with a wounded leg, the effects of a cannonball that had splintered the deck of his ship. He later described the wound as "a grievous blow in my leg, interlaced and deformed with splinters."[6] Raleigh spent the next few days picking splinters from his leg, and he walked with a limp and a stick for the

The Revenge *was a thirty-four-gun ship of 441 tons that served as Sir Francis Drake's flagship in the battle against the Spanish Armada. In 1591, under Sir Richard Grenville, the* Revenge *battled an overwhelming Spanish fleet for fifteen hours before foundering in a storm off the Azores.*

rest of his life. He emerged from battle at Cadíz as the true hero of a great English victory.

In the battle's aftermath, English troops sacked the town, but the real prize of Cadíz—the rich merchant ships still moored in the harbor—escaped the raiders. Howard, Essex, and Vere opted to offer the ships for ransom. King Philip would have none of that, however. He ordered the entire merchant fleet to be burned and scuttled. The raiders could only watch in dismay as enormous riches slipped from their grasp and sank to the bottom of the harbor. The marauders headed home to claim a great military victory, but not a doubloon richer for their trouble.

When the English fleet arrived home in early August, the people hailed Essex as the hero of Cadíz—but insiders knew the true hero was Raleigh. A year later, Queen Elizabeth welcomed him back to

James I of England, shown here in his regal finery, was the former James VI of Scotland. The son of Mary, Queen of Scots, James ascended to the English throne upon the death of Elizabeth I in 1603.

her court and restored his place as captain of the guard. In 1599, she sent Essex to Ireland as her lord lieutenant. She later stripped him of his offices for failing to quell a rebel uprising and for deserting his post when he attempted to vindicate himself.

In February 1601, Essex tried and failed to raise the populace of London in revolt against the queen. Elizabeth had him tried and convicted for treason. One of the great rivalries in history ended at the executioner's block on February 25, 1601. Raleigh, as captain of the Queen's Guard, witnessed the execution of Essex in the Tower of London.

Raleigh partially regained his welcome at court but not his former wealth, prestige, and power. He continued to serve his aging queen until she fell ill and died on March 24, 1603, just shy of seventy. Three days later, King James VI of Scotland—son of the late Mary, Queen of Scots—began his southward journey to assume the throne of England as James I. The world of Sir Walter Raleigh was about to change forever.

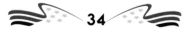

The Spanish Armada

Elizabeth I ascended to the throne during troubled religious times in 1558 but managed to keep England at peace for thirty years. One of her first acts as queen was to restore the Protestant Church of England as the official state religion. Philip II of Spain, a devout Catholic, resented her action. His resentment grew with repeated attacks on Spanish ships by English Sea Rovers like Sir Francis Drake. He finally decided to curb the English sea attacks and restore Catholicism in England. After years of preparation, Philip assembled a great fleet of ships to mount an invasion of England. The fleet came to be known as the Spanish—or Grand—Armada.

In late July 1588, the Spanish Armada of some 130 warships (left) sailed into the English Channel under the command of the Duke of Medina-Sidonia. Its mission was to seize control of the Channel so that Spanish troops led by the Alessandro Farnese, the Duke of Parma, could invade the island nation. Elizabeth countered with a much smaller fleet of some ninety-four warships and mixed commercial vessels led by Lord Howard of Effingham. The ensuing sea battle raged from July 21 to 29, 1588.

Beginning on July 21, the smaller, faster English gunships attacked a crescent-shaped line of heavier, slower Spanish warships intermittently for a week. On July 28, Medina led many of his ships into the sheltering harbor of Calais, France. He found no safe harbor there. English fireships—small ships filled with combustible materials and set afire—forced Medina's panicking ships back into the Channel. Sir Francis Drake and others gave chase and caught the Spaniards off Gravelines, a port in northern France. In an eight-hour battle, the English sank three Spanish ships and sent five more aground and on fire.

When the English ran out of ammunition, the Armada fled north around Scotland. Many Spanish ships were wrecked in the rough waters. Fewer than half of Medina's ships returned safely to Spain. The English did not lose a single ship in the epic sea battle.

Sir Walter consoles his beloved spouse after their fall from grace at Queen Elizabeth's court. Bess shared Raleigh's quarters in the Tower of London during much of his thirteen-year confinement. Their son Wat lived in separate quarters in this famous fortress on the north bank of the Thames River.

CHAPTER
5

Even Stars Must Fall

Sir Walter Raleigh had often spoken out against the succession of Scotland's James VI to the throne of England as James I. Still, he intended to serve him well. On May 3, 1603, he rushed to meet the new king at the estate of his supposed friend, Robert Cecil. Their meeting represented a study in contrasts. At about age fifty, Raleigh remained a handsome figure, physically fit despite his limp, and fashionably attired. James, at thirty-eight years old, with straggly beard, shabby dress, and awkward bearing, appeared less than regal. The king greeted Raleigh with a bad pun that implied he wasn't much of a gentleman: "Mon, I have heard 'rawley' of you!"[1] Their relationship, helped by the treachery of Cecil and others, went downhill from there. With Elizabeth dead, Raleigh stood virtually at the mercy of a host of envious enemies.

Encouraged by Raleigh's enemies, James I acted at once to strip Raleigh of his rank and holdings. He withdrew the licenses and monopolies Elizabeth had granted him and replaced him as captain of the guard. He revoked his lease on Durham House. Lastly, the king dismissed Walter as governor of Jersey, his last appointed office from Elizabeth. In July, the Privy Council questioned Raleigh about what he knew of a plot to dethrone the new king. He maintained he knew nothing of it. Before the week ended, he found himself a prisoner in the Tower of London on charges of treason.

Raleigh was brought before the Court of the King's Bench at Winchester on November 17, 1603. The charges against him were read: "That he did conspire, and go about to deprive the King of his Government; to raise up Sedition [rebellion] within the Realm; to alter Religion, to bring in the Roman Superstition, and to procure Foreign enemies to invade the Kingdoms."[2] The charges continued at length, accusing him of plotting with Lord Cobham to advance Arabella Stuart, the king's cousin, to the throne. Raleigh denied all charges and acted in his own defense. His ensuing trial—considered a farce by most scholars—resulted in a swift conviction. The court sentenced him to a gruesome death, but the king stayed his execution. Instead, Raleigh was to be sent to the Tower of London and confined as a condemned but unexecuted traitor without any legal existence.

Walter spent the next thirteen years in the Tower of London, largely in the Bloody Tower. For much of that time, his wife, Bess, resided with him and his son Wat occupied other quarters within the sprawling royal fortress. Bess gave birth to a third son, Carew, in 1605. During his years of confinement, Sir Walter devoted himself to scientific studies and experiments and to his writing. Already an accomplished author and poet, he started writing his famous *History of the World*, but he succeeded in advancing it only to 146 BCE. He also tutored the king's son Henry, Prince of Wales, until the prince's death from cholera in 1612.

Throughout his imprisonment, Raleigh stayed true to his dream of someday finding El Dorado. Finally, in 1616, he persuaded James I to release him for a return expedition to South America. To gain his freedom, Raleigh promised to bring back gold from a mine he claimed to have discovered on his earlier expedition. The king's extravagance had severely strained the royal treasury. Accordingly, the prospect of great riches intrigued him. He granted his permission for a second expedition, but he warned Raleigh not to intrude on any Spanish territory under penalty of death. James did not want further trouble with Spain.

Raleigh spent more than a year preparing for the voyage. On June 12, 1617, he at last sailed out of Plymouth with seven ships and three pinnaces (small vessels of about twenty tons). At year's

Raleigh with his son Walter. Bess gave birth to Walter—who was known as Wat—at Sherborne Castle in 1594. Wat followed in his father's adventurous footsteps until he was killed in a skirmish with Spaniards while searching for El Dorado.

end, they reached the mouth of the Orinoco, where fate again thwarted Raleigh's quest for the golden city. A fever rendered him too sick to proceed. All agreed that Raleigh should stay behind in Trinidad.

In his place, Raleigh sent five small vessels up the Orinoco under the command of Lawrence Keymis. He told his most trusted captain to proceed upriver to the mine area at Caroní junction. Most important, Keymis was to avoid hostile action with any Spaniards he might encounter along the way. Keymis and his party, including Raleigh's son Wat, set out on their search for gold with the best of intentions. At San Thomé (now Ciudad Guayana or San Tomé de Guayana), however, Keymis found his way blocked by a Spanish fortification. Accounts of what actually happened vary, but a fiery encounter ensued that claimed the lives of Wat Raleigh, another Englishman, and the governor of San Thomé.

Afterward, Keymis led his party on upriver. He eventually returned—without having found an ounce of gold—to Trinidad and a harsh dressing down from Raleigh. The distraught Keymis shot himself. Raleigh, anguished over the loss of his son, again headed home empty-handed.

Back in England, Raleigh found the king incensed over the expedition's encounter with the Spaniards, a hostile action that he had strictly forbidden. He used the incident to reinstate Raleigh's original death sentence on charges of treason. At 8:00 A.M. on October 28, 1618, Raleigh received a summons to appear before the King's Bench at Westminster to hear the final order for his execution. He stood before the court an hour later.

After the reading of Raleigh's earlier conviction, Attorney General Sir Henry Yelverton commented, "He hath been as a star at which the world has gazed; but stars may fall, nay, they must fall when they trouble the sphere wherein they abide."[3] Then, on behalf of his Majesty, he called for Raleigh's execution. Moments later, Lord Chief Justice Sir Henry Montague declared, "Execution granted."[4] The execution was scheduled for the next morning in Westminster's Old Palace Yard.

Raleigh spent his last evening in the Abbey Gatehouse (prison), comforting Bess and making peace with all things earthly and divine. Bess left shortly after midnight. In the morning, he dressed in his customary splendor. He wore a satin doublet (jacket), an embroidered waistcoat (vest), black taffeta breeches, and colored silk stockings. An embroidered night cap and a black velvet cloak completed his attire. He arrived at the Old Palace Yard at about eight o'clock on the morning of October 29, 1618. A crowd of onlookers had already gathered to witness the impending spectacle. Two sheriffs led him to the scaffold.

Raleigh addressed the crowd for half an hour in a final effort to clear his name. He concluded, saying, "So I take my leave of

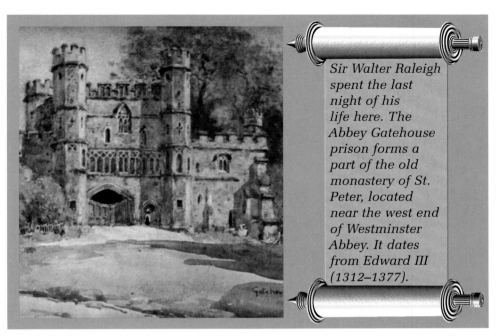

Sir Walter Raleigh spent the last night of his life here. The Abbey Gatehouse prison forms a part of the old monastery of St. Peter, located near the west end of Westminster Abbey. It dates from Edward III (1312–1377).

you all, making peace with God."[5] He then turned to the executioner and asked to see the ax. Fingering the blade, he said, "This is a sharp medicine, but a physician for all diseases."[6] Refusing a blindfold, Raleigh placed his head on the block and signaled his executioner to strike. The executioner delayed. "Strike man," Raleigh commanded, "strike!"[7] The executioner's ax fell once, then once again.

Sir Walter's lips were still moving in prayer when his head toppled to the ground. The executioner lifted the severed head by the hair and held it high for all to see. A soft moan issued forth from the crowd. One voice cried out, "We have never had such a head cut off."[8] And so fell one of the brightest stars of the Elizabethan era.

Sir Walter Raleigh died as he had lived—bravely. He was a visionary with great ambition and lofty aims, who dreamed of colonizing both North and South America. Whether from the press of circumstance or from his own shortcomings, he never realized his dream. In either case, he played an important role in the development of early America. He was beyond question one of the dominant figures of his time.

The Plots Against the King

The plots against James I of England that ultimately cost Sir Walter Raleigh and others their lives were known as the Bye and Main Plots. The Bye (or "Surprising") Plot was also called The Treason of the Priests. It began with two Catholic priests, William Watson and Francis Clarke. With the help of hired swordsmen Sir Griffin Markham and Anthony Copley, the priests conspired to seize or "surprise" James I and members of his Privy Council. They planned to hold their prisoners in the Tower of London and pressure them into elevating Catholics into positions of power.

At about the same time, a group of Protestant conspirators set in motion a plot of their own. The Main Plot was led by Lord Grey of Wilton and George Brooke, brother of Lord Cobham. Both men held grudges against Lord (Robert) Cecil, 1st Earl of Salisbury, the king's chief minister. Grey knew of the Bye Plot but took no part in it. His scheme was much more complex than the Catholic plot. Simply put, however, the Main Plot also called for the seizure of the king.

Lord Grey, a former soldier, was to raise a regiment to surround James I and force him to give up his throne in favor of the king's cousin, Arabella Stuart (left). Raleigh became implicated in the plot because of his friendship with Lord Cobham. Raleigh was also charged with urging Arabella to seek financial aid from the king of Spain.

Agents of the king soon uncovered the Bye Plot. They arrested the two priests and Copley, and the priests were executed. Copley's examination led to the arrest of Markham and Grey. Brooke was also arrested. To save his own life, Brooke implicated his brother in the second plot. To save himself, Cobham, in turn, incriminated Raleigh. Raleigh denied all charges against him. His trial is widely thought to have been a sham, but the absolute truth about the plots against the king will likely remain uncertain.

Chapter Notes

Chapter 1   Prisoner of the King
1. Raleigh Trevelyan, *Sir Walter Raleigh* (New York: Henry Holt, 2002), p. 387.
2. William Stebbing, *Sir Walter Ralegh: A Biography* (Honolulu: University Press of the Pacific, 2004), p. 240.
3. Ibid.
4. Luminarium: *Sir Walter Raleigh Bids Farewell to His Wife a Few Hours Before He Expects to Be Executed* (**http://www.luminarium.org/renlit/raleghfarewell.htm**), p. 1.
5. Ibid., p. 2.
6. John W. Shirley, *Sir Walter Ralegh and the New World* (Raleigh: North Carolina Division of Archives and History, 1997), p. 106.

Chapter 2   Early Life and Fortune
1. Raleigh Trevelyan, *Sir Walter Raleigh* (New York: Henry Holt, 2002), p. 12.
2. Ibid., p. xv.
3. Peter Kemp, ed., *The Oxford Companion to Ships and the Sea* (New York: Oxford University Press, 1988), p. 687.
4. William Stebbing, *Sir Walter Ralegh: A Biography* (Honolulu: University Press of the Pacific, 2004), p. 15.

Chapter 3   Favorite at Court
1. John W. Shirley, *Sir Walter Ralegh and the New World* (Raleigh: North Carolina Division of Archives and History, 1997), p. 18.
2. Ibid.
3. Ibid., p. 19.
4. Lee Miller, *Roanoke: Solving the Mystery of the Lost Colony* (New York: Penguin Books, 2002), p. 139.
5. J. H. Parry, *Romance of the Sea* (Washington, D.C.: National Geographic Society, 1981), p. 164.
6. Richard Hakluyt, *Voyages and Discoveries: The Principal Navigations, Voyages, Traffiques and Discoveries of the English Nation* (Penguin Classics. Edited, abridged, and introduced by Jack Beeching. New York: Penguin Books, 1985), pp. 241–242.
7. Roger Whiting, *The Enterprise of England: The Spanish Armada* (New York: St. Martin's Press, 1995), p. 79.

Chapter 4   Adventurer at Large
1. Richard Hakluyt, *Voyages and Discoveries: The Principal Navigations, Voyages, Traffiques and Discoveries of the English Nation* (Penguin Classics. Edited, abridged, and introduced by Jack Beeching. New York: Penguin Books, 1985), p. 395.
2. Ibid., p. 401.
3. Ibid., p. 410.
4. William Stebbing, *Sir Walter Ralegh: A Biography* (Honolulu: University Press of the Pacific, 2004), p. 125.
5. John W. Shirley, *Sir Walter Ralegh and the New World* (Raleigh: North Carolina Division of Archives and History, 1997), p. 101.
6. Raleigh Trevelyan, *Sir Walter Raleigh* (New York: Henry Holt, 2002), p. 277.

Chapter 5   Even Stars Must Fall
1. John W. Shirley, *Sir Walter Ralegh and the New World* (Raleigh: North Carolina Division of Archives and History, 1997), p. 104.
2. Barbara O'Sullivan, *The King's Quinto: The Life and Times of Sir Walter Raleigh (1552–1618)* (Baltimore: PublishAmerica, 2003), p. 134.
3. William Stebbing, *Sir Walter Ralegh: A Biography* (Honolulu: University Press of the Pacific, 2004), p. 366.
4. Ibid., p. 367.
5. Christopher Smith, *Sir Walter Raleigh* (**http://britannica.com/bios/raleigh/**), part 19, p. 2.
6. O'Sullivan, p. 203.
7. Smith, part 19, p. 2.
8. Raleigh Trevelyan, *Sir Walter Raleigh* (New York: Henry Holt, 2002), p. 552.

Chronology

1554	(possibly 1552) Born at Hayes Barton in East Budleigh, Salterton, Devon, England
1569	Fights with the Huguenots (French Protestants) in France's Wars of Religion
1572	Attends Oriel College, Oxford
1575	Studies law at Middle Temple, London
1578	Joins Sir Humphrey Gilbert on a "voyage of discovery"
1580–81	Fights as an army captain against rebels in Ireland
1582	Becomes favorite of Queen Elizabeth I
1583	Acquires trade privileges and rights to colonize America
1584	Serves in Parliament for the first time, where he frequently sits during the 1590s
1584–89	Sponsors several attempts to establish a colony near Roanoke Island (in present-day North Carolina)
1585	Knighted; named warden of the stannaries (Cornish tin mines), lieutenant of Cornwall, and vice admiral of Devon and Cornwall
1586	Helps to uncover the Babington Plot
1587	Appointed captain of the Queen's Guard
1588	Takes part in the defense of England and defeat of the Spanish Armada
1591	Secretly marries Elizabeth ("Bess") Throckmorton, a lady-in-waiting to Elizabeth I
1592	Linked adversely with "School of Night"; he and Bess are imprisoned for their secret marriage by Elizabeth I, then are banished from her court
1593	Retires with Bess to Sherborne; sits occasionally in Parliament
1594	Bess gives birth to a son, Walter, known as Wat
1595	Leads expedition to present-day Venezuela in search of El Dorado, the fabled city of gold; describes expedition in The Discoverie of . . . Guiana
1597	Accompanies rival Robert Devereux, 2nd Earl of Essex, in a raid against the Spanish fleet and fortifications at Cádiz; Raleigh wounded; rivalry with Essex heightens
1599	Elizabeth restores his place on her court
1600–03	Serves as governor of Jersey
1601	Witnesses execution of Essex
1603	Elizabeth I dies; James I, her successor, convicts and imprisons Raleigh on false charges of conspiring against him
1605	Son Carew Raleigh is born
1616	Released from prison to resume search for El Dorado; mission aborted after unsuccessful raid (against the king's orders) on Spanish fort at San Thomé; Walter's son, Wat, killed in the fighting
1618	Is executed on October 29

Timeline in History

1502	Christopher Columbus embarks on his fourth and final voyage to the Caribbean.
1513	Vasco Nuñez de Balboa crosses Isthmus of Panama and discovers Pacific Ocean.
1517	Martin Luther posts Ninety-five Theses for reformation of church practices.
1521	Hernándo Cortés completes conquest of Aztec Empire in present-day Mexico; Ferdinand Magellan is slain in the Philippines.
1522	Juan Sebastián de Elcano returns to Spain to complete the first around-the-world voyage, begun under Magellan's command.
1530	Portugal begins to colonize lands in Brazil.
1534	Jacques Cartier explores the Gulf of St. Lawrence; Henry VIII of England forms Protestant Church of England with himself at its head.
1536	Francisco Pizarro concludes conquest of Incas in today's Peru.
1547	Henry VIII dies and is succeeded by Edward VI.
1553	Edward VI dies; Mary I succeeds him.
1556	Philip II ascends to the Spanish throne and reigns until his death in 1598.
1558	Mary I dies; Elizabeth I succeeds her and reigns for the next forty-five years.
1568–70	France's Third War of Religion is fought between the Catholics and Huguenots.
1571	Spanish forces of Philip II defeat the Ottomans at the Battle of Lepanto.
1580	Spain annexes Portugal.
1583	Sir Humphrey Gilbert died at sea after claiming Newfoundland for the queen.
1587	Elizabeth I orders the execution of Mary Stuart (Queen of Scots).
1588	England defeats the Spanish Armada.
1607	First enduring English settlement in North America is established at Jamestown.
1618	Thirty Years' War between Protestants and Catholics in Europe begins.
1620	Puritan Separatists (Pilgrims) on the Mayflower land at Plymouth.
1625	Dutch colonists found New Amsterdam on the island of Manhattan; reign of England's James I ends; Charles I succeeds him.
1640	Portugal regains its independence from Spain.
1649	Authoritarian reign of England's Charles I ends with his execution.
1653–58	Oliver Cromwell rules England as Lord Protector of the Commonwealth.

Further Reading

For Young Adults

Aronson, Marc. *Sir Walter Raleigh and the Quest for El Dorado.* Boston: Houghton Mifflin Company, 2000.

Chippendale, Neil. *Sir Walter Raleigh and the Search for El Dorado.* Explorers of New Worlds Series. Broomall, PA: Chelsea House Publishers, 2001.

Larkin, Tanya. *Sir Walter Raleigh.* Famous Explorers Series. New York: Rosen Publishing Group, 2003.

Marcovitz, Hal. *Sir Walter Raleigh.* Explorers of New Worlds Series. Broomall, PA: Chelsea House Publishers, 2002.

Olson, Steven P. *Sir Walter Raleigh: Explorer for the Court of Queen Elizabeth.* Library of Explorers and Exploration. New York: Rosen Publishing Group, 2003.

Works Consulted

Bohlander, Richard E. (editor). *World Explorers and Discoverers.* New York: Da Capo Press, 1998.

Daniels, Patricia S., and Stephen G. Hyslop. *Almanac of World History.* Washington, D.C.: National Geographic Society, 2003.

Foss, Michael. *Undreamed Shores: England's Wasted Empire in America.* London: Phoenix Press, 2000.

Hakluyt, Richard. *Voyages and Discoveries: The Principal Navigations, Voyages, Traffiques and Discoveries of the English Nation.* Penguin Classics. Edited, abridged, and introduced by Jack Beeching. New York: Penguin Books, 1985.

Kelsey, Harry. *Sir Francis Drake: The Queen's Pirate.* New Haven: Yale University Press, 2000.

Kemp, Peter (editor). *The Oxford Companion to Ships and the Sea.* New York: Oxford University Press, 1988.

Miller, Lee. Roanoke: *Solving the Mystery of the Lost Colony.* New York: Penguin Books, 2002.

Milton, Giles. *Big Chief Elizabeth: The Adventures and Fate of the First English Colonists in America.* New York: Farrar, Straus and Giroux, 2000.

Nicholl, Charles. *The Creature in the Map: A Journey to El Dorado.* New York: William Morrow and Company, 1995.

O'Sullivan, Barbara. *The King's Quinto: The Life and Times of Sir Walter Raleigh (1552–1618).* Baltimore: PublishAmerica, 2003.

Parry, J. H. *Romance of the Sea.* Washington, DC: National Geographic Society, 1981.

Shirley, John W. *Sir Walter Ralegh and the New World.* Raleigh: North Carolina Division of Archives and History, 1997.

Stebbing, William. *Sir Walter Ralegh: A Biography.* Honolulu: University Press of the Pacific, 2004.

Trevelyan, Raleigh. *Sir Walter Raleigh.* New York: Henry Holt, 2002.

Whiting, Roger. *The Enterprise of England: The Spanish Armada.* New York: St. Martin's Press, 1995.

Woodman, Richard. *The History of the Ship: The Comprehensive Story of Seafaring from the Earliest Times to the Present Day.* New York: Lyons Press, 1997.

On the Internet

British Explorers: Sir Walter Raleigh, of Hayes Barton, Woodbury Common
http://www.britishexplorers.com/woodbury/raleigh.html

Modern History Sourcebook: Sir Walter Raleigh (1554–1618): The Discovery of Guiana, 1595
http://www.fordham.edu/halsall/mod/1595raleigh-guiana.html

State Library of North Carolina: First English Settlement in the New World
http://statelibrary.dcr.state.nc.us/nc/ncsites/English1.htm

Luminarium: Sir Walter Raleigh Bids Farewell to His Wife a Few Hours before He Expects to Be Executed
http://www.luminarium.org/renlit/ralegh-farewell.htm

Christopher Smith: Sir Walter Raleigh
http://britannica.com/bios/raleigh/

Glossary

barbarous (BAR-buh-rus)
Uncivilized; cruel.

bungle (BUNG-gul)
To spoil by lack of skill; to attempt and fail clumsily.

Caroni (kah-roh-NEE)
River in southeast Venezuela.

concentric (kon-SEN-trik)
Having the same center, as concentric circles.

courtier (KOR-tee-yur)
One who attends royalty at court.

countermand (KOWN-ter-mand)
To cancel a command or order.

Cumaná (koo-ma-NAH)
Seaport city on the Venezuelan coast; now believed to be the oldest existing European settlement in South America.

doubloon (duh-BLOON)
A Spanish gold coin.

El Dorado (el-doh-RAH-doh)
The fabled city of gold thought to exist in South America; called Manoa by native peoples.

embrasure (em-BRAY-zhur)
An opening in a wall for a gun.

flota (FLOH-tuh)
A fleet of merchant ships escorted by warships.

Guiana (gee-AH-nah)
Region in South America between the Orinoco, Negro, and Amazon Rivers and the Atlantic Ocean.

heathen (HEE-then)
A person who does not believe in any of the world's great religions, especially one who is not a Christian, Jew, or Muslim.

heresy (HAIR-uh-see)
Holding a religious belief contrary to church doctrine.

Huguenots (HYOO-guh-not)
French Protestants of the fifteenth and sixteenth centuries.

imminent (IH-mih-nent)
About to occur, or likely to occur at any moment.

imp
A small demon or mischievous child.

lofty
Very tall, towering; noble thoughts or aims.

quell (KWEL)
To suppress or curb.

menagerie (meh-NAA-juh-ree)
A collection of wild animals in captivity for exhibition.

nimble (NIM-bul)
Able to move (or think) quickly; agile.

Orinoco (or-ee-NOH-koh)
A river in present-day Venezuela.

regal (REE-gul)
Like or fit for a king.

scuttle (SKUH-tul)
To deliberately sink a ship by cutting holes in the bottom.

sprawl
Spread out in an irregular or straggling way.

thwart
To prevent something that is intended, as a plan or plot.

yen
A longing or yearning.

Index

Anne Aucher   18
Aubrey, John   16, 22
Azores   18, 21, 23, 25, 26
Babington Plot   23, 44
Bourbon, Louis de (Prince of Condé)
   14
Boleyn, Anne   11, 16, 19
Carew, George   16
Catherine of Aragon   14
Cecil, Lord Robert (1st Earl of Salisbury)
   31, 37, 42
Cecil, Sir William (Lord Burghley)   19
Champernowne, Charles   16
Champernowne, Henry   14
Cobham, Lord (Henry Brooke)   8, 9, 42
Drake, Sir Francis   13, 17, 24, 25, 27,
   35
Dudley, Robert, Earl of Leicester   16,
   17
Edward VI   14
Elizabeth I   16, 17, 19, 22, 23, 24, 25,
   26, 31, 33, 34, 35, 37, 41
Essex, 2nd Earl of (Devereux, Robert)
   19, 24, 25, 26, 31, 33, 34
Falcon   18
Gilbert, Sir Humphrey   13, 16, 17, 18,
   21, 23
Grenville, Sir Richard   26, 27, 32, 33
Grey, Lord Thomas   8, 9, 21, 22, 42
Henry, Prince of Wales   38
Henry VII   16
Henry VIII   11, 14, 16, 19
Howard, Lord of Effingham   24, 35
Huguenots (French Protestants)   14, 15
Ireland   18, 21, 22, 25, 31, 34
James I   7, 8, 10, 34, 37, 38, 42
Keymis, Lawrence   29, 39, 40
Languedoc   15
Markham, Sir Griffin   8, 9, 42
Mary I   12, 14, 16, 17, 19
Mary, Queen of Scots   19, 20, 24, 34
Middle Temple   15, 16
Moncontour   15
Montague, Sir Henry   40
More, Sir Thomas   11
Newfoundland   23
Oriel College   15, 16
Philip II   12, 14, 17, 19, 24, 25, 35
Popham, Sir John   7
Raleigh, Carew (brother)   13
Raleigh, Carew (son)   38

Raleigh, Damerei (son)   24
Raleigh, Elizabeth ("Bess") (wife)   9,
   24, 26, 36, 38, 40
Raleigh, Katherine (mother)   13, 14
Raleigh, Margaret (sister)   13
Raleigh, Walter (father)   13
Raleigh, Walter   6, 14, 19, 23, 26, 28,
   34, 39, 42
   Accused of atheism   26
   Babington Plot   23, 24
   Banished from court of
      Elizabeth I   26
   Birth of   13
   Cadíz raid   31, 32, 33
   Captain of Queen's Guard   6, 7,
      8, 24
   Colony at Roanoke Island   23, 26
   Confinement   9, 10, 11, 26, 36,
      37, 38
   Education of   15–16
   El Dorado   29, 30, 31, 38, 39
   Execution   10, 40, 41
   Favorite at queen's court   19, 21,
      22
   Friendship with Edmund Spenser
      25
   In France's Third War of Religion
      14
   In Irish Rebellion   21, 22
   Knighted by Elizabeth I   23
   Married Elizabeth ("Bess")
      Throckmorton   24
   Rivalry with Essex   24, 25, 34
   Titles conferred upon   23
   Trade licenses and monopolies
      granted   22
   Tried for treason   7, 8, 37, 38
   Wounded   32
   Writings   26, 30, 38
Raleigh, Walter ("Wat") (son)   26, 38,
   39, 40
Revenge   26, 32, 33
Spanish (Grand) Armada   19, 24, 25,
   27, 31, 32, 35
Stuart, Arabella   38, 42
Topiawari   28, 30
Tower of London   6, 10, 11, 26, 34, 37,
   38, 42
Walsingham, Sir Francis   22, 23, 26
Winchester, England   7, 8, 10, 38